CBD: For Healing Opioid Addiction

CBD: For Healing Opioid Addiction

Jose Jones

To order additional copies of this book, contact:
Xlibris
844-714-8691
www.Xlibris.com
Orders@Xlibris.com
836984

CONTENTS

CBD FOR HEALING OPIOID ADDICTION

THIS HANDBOOK WAS written with the intention of providing useful information to families and friends regarding our country's opioid (synthetic and natural) addiction epidemic. Presently and unfortunately we are experiencing approximately 90,000 overdose deaths per year with people using these drugs. Specifically, this handbook covers the following useful information: the opioid addiction history, ancient healing of addiction, history and research regarding the use of cannabidiol (CBD) for treating opioid addiction, our attempt to solve the epidemic through incarceration, healing and laws governing CBD, recommended doses of CBD for addiction treatment and other illnesses, the roles pharmaceutical companies have played in the production of these synthetic opioids, stories of several families and how they handled family members with this addiction sickness, and much more.

It must be noted that this handbook was written by a simple family member with many years of experience in dealing with family members and friends that have been plagued with the sickness of opioid addiction.

Do note that this booklet does not provide medical advice. What it does do is share positive CBD use experiences from family members with opioid addiction in their families, and meaningful CBD research findings from well-known researchers.

ACKNOWLEDGMENTS

I AM MOST APPRECIATIVE of the encouragement and motivation and inspiration I received from my wife, daughters, son, brothers, sister, and family+ + + + +. Also a special thank you to Bobby for his tireless editing and ideas. This primer handbook could not have been possible without the input from Cameron, Frank, and Melvin. Most of all, credit needs to be given to a multitude of families that through the years to the present time have never given up and have more than happily been willing to unselfishly share their many stories of their fights to defeat the plaguing sickness of opioid addiction.

The strength of the American family, especially mothers, and the use of natural healing like CBD are the *real answers to this mentioned epidemic.* America has the science, and we know that *treatment works, we just need more of it!*

CHAPTER I

Some Important Segments of the Drug Addiction Treatment History in America

WORLD WAR II ended, but the beginning of the drug epidemic in America continued, and to a large extent, worsened. Once Prohibition was over, illegal alcohol was not profitable anymore; therefore, many organized crime groups turned to trafficking heroin/opioids and marijuana. Tremendous amounts of soldiers coming back from World War II had been wounded in the war, and made for very lucrative markets for the pushers/dealers as they transitioned from legal army-issued morphine to street heroin and other opioids.

There had always been heroin addicts in every major city of America, but most of this addiction was minor and underground. The returning wounded soldiers landed back home self-medicating with heroin, and all of a sudden the underground heroin addiction problem floated to the top. Almost overnight, every major city in America had a neighborhood and/or street where the heroin addicts connected and bought heroin and/or other opioids and marijuana and hung out, and many were veterans. A perfect example of this phenomenon was the city of El Paso, Texas, where most of the heroin/opioid addicts gravitated to El Paso Street in the downtown area and made it their turf. The street pushers/dealers also joined the addicts, where they would deal their heroin/opioid products. Because of the purity of the heroin of the time, most heroin/opioid addicts would have to inject or shoot up a quarter of a gram four times per day, which was very advantageous for the pusher/dealer, because this meant that they would sell more of their product. Opioid addiction at this time also developed its own subculture, which included its own language, customs, and rules. A good example of this was that in their slang, heroin was called "chiva" (goat) in Spanish and "horse" in English. These slang words related to the kick or rush of the heroin as it entered the body through the blood vessel, which usually was the left arm—at least, until those vessels collapsed, then they would search in every part of the body until they found another good vein.

Yes, some would detox themselves from the heroin/opioid (cold turkey) using marijuana (THC/CBD) and whatever opioid medication they could get hold of. As part of their own detox they also drank a lot of beer. This addiction was morally deviant by choice, as it was known at the time that it created its own morals, values, hierarchy, and language. The street pusher/dealer controlled the streets, while the street heroin/opioid addicts became the customers, and to an extent, slaves to the drug. Opioid addiction at this time was still not considered an Illness.

The street heroin/opioid addicts soon learned that they had started using heroin/opioids to deal with medical pain or were searching for a high, but instead most ended up using the drugs to avoid painful withdrawal symptoms and simply to function somewhat normally for several hours until the next injection (fix). Most of the street pushers/dealers, in their greedy way of thinking, would dilute the heroin with substances such as sugar and so on to increase the amount, thus increasing their profits. This caused many problems for the street addict, such as having to inject more often, sometimes four and five times a day because they would start getting sick shortly after the injection rather than it lasting for four to five hours. Since they were injecting (fixing, shooting) more often they were forced to share needles, and this caused many diseases that would be passed down from addict to addict. A major problem arose as the heroin was being diluted with poisonous substances such as strychnine, Drano, and other deadly substances.

The start of the opioid epidemic created many health issues in America. In the meantime, many heroin/opioid addicts in their attempts to self-medicate relied heavily on marijuana (CBD), pain pills, sleeping pills, beer, foreign opioid pills, and natural remedies. The addicts soon found out that hemp plant extract and indoor-grown marijuana (where the flower blossomed to the max) was stronger and more helpful in their self-detox.

At this time the heroin/opioid addict did not know that it was the cannabidiol (CBD) in the hemp that was making them feel good and taking away the heroin/opioid withdrawal pains, shakes, nausea, anxiety, and all the other withdrawal signs and symptoms. The addicts also did not know that the medicinal liquid coming in from Brazil, China, and Canada was CBD. All they knew was that it was making them feel good. In essence, other than methadone, CBD can be considered one of the first medications used in the self-treatment of heroin addiction. During withdrawal sickness, it was very common for the addict to say, "I'll be alright after I smoke a joint and take my little magic potion."

The forties and fifties left us with the start of a drug epidemic, and the sixties were brought in by the war in Vietnam, where opium and marijuana were in abundance and very affordable. It was very common for American soldiers to purchase from native Vietnamese a five-pound bag of opium-laced marijuana for a carton of American Salem menthol cigarettes. The rule was you do not get loaded (intoxicated) when you are on patrol, but when you come back to base camp you all can light up or shoot up (inject), and the majority did. This gave birth to a new form of heroin opioid addict. An addict that could withstand opioids that were strong and concentrated. It also gave birth to the "combat zone" pusher (hustler) and to illegal underground, clandestine overdose treatment sites within the combat zone, where soldiers could bring their overdosed friends for help. These clinics would charge an upfront fee whether the treatment worked or not. The overdose treatment protocol usually consisted of coffee enemas, an IV with dextrose (sugar), and gradual increments of French amphetamines bought on the black market. And lastly, inflicting pain in the sternum, armpits in increasing episodes until the soldier would stop foaming at the mouth, wake up. And at that moment he would rapidly be removed from the stretcher to make room for the next one, who was usually waiting to be revived. Of course, it was guaranteed that nothing would appear in the soldier's record, and if the soldier died in the process, the record would show "Died in Action," because, after all, it was very clear that the enemy was using the locally grown opium as a very effective weapon in the war.

The Vietnam War not only exponentially increased heroin/opioid addiction in America, but it also created a new type of heroin/opioid addict. An addict that could withstand high-grade heroin/opioid, and who was willing to mix it up with cocaine (speedballing), with amphetamines, barbiturates, marijuana, analgesics (pain killers), and yes, even hallucinogenics like LSD, STP, and other laboratory synthetics.

The Vietnam protestors era brought in the laboratory created hallucinogenics, and made marijuana quite popular and widely accepted. For all purposes, the "hippie," "flower children," and "free love" movements of the sixties brought in the drug culture to mainstream America. At the time, it almost seem like everybody wanted to smoke marijuana (grass/weed) and go on at least one trip of LSD (acid).

As expected, when the drug culture hit mainstream America, the federal government responded by declaring a war on drugs. The war was declared on two fronts. These were 1.) incarceration and 2.) rehabilitation. In their infinite wisdom, the government decided that the majority of the funding would go to incarceration, while rehabilitation received token resources. The mentality of the time was "let's incarcerate our way out of this one." However, the incarceration mentality did not work in that the problem got worse. In the meantime, heroin/opioid addiction blossomed like never before in that China, Mexico, and other countries saw the huge American demand and they became very sophisticated "profitable suppliers." There were no drug cartels in the sixties and early seventies. There were only addict supported and protected "shooting galleries" and "connections," where you could walk in, buy the heroin, cook it (prepare for injection) and inject it, wait for the rush (to make sure you were not going to overdose), and then walk out—usually with a week's supply, only to return sooner.

Methadone, an opioid treatment medication, had been used before with some success. Therefore, in the late sixties and early seventies the federal government started funding methadone clinics in almost every major city in America. Methadone is a popular medication used for opioid treatment, whether it be for maintenance or detox. It is supposed to assist opioid addicts with the pain and overall discomfort of withdrawal, and curb the craving. Even though methadone was and has been somewhat successful, it was too little too late, because by the eighties and nineties America counted millions of opioid addicts, mainly of heroin and synthetic opioids.

Furthermore, by that time the court system in America somehow also got addicted to the mentality of jailing them and throwing the key away. This caused the prison system to balloon, and almost overnight the federal prison population went from 20,000 to almost 200,000. At this time private business saw an opportunity and started developing private prisons and making sizeable profits, and of course this politized the incarceration front to solving the opioid problem.

Presently, America counts over 50 million addicts, many of whom are addicted to heroin/opioids and the latest craze of synthetics, which are killing over 90,000 Americans per year. Also cited by the United Nations Office of Drug and Crimes, there are 162 million to 324 million people in the world using drugs, and approximately 183,000 are dying per year due to the drug use.

Pharmaceutical corporations are getting sued and paying millions of dollars, and are being accused of causing the overdose deaths due to synthetic opioids. But will this be enough to solve the drug addiction epidemic in America? The answer is probably no. A big part of the answer is the development of new and innovative education, prevention, treatment, intervention, and recovery models, and of course, reviving street models that have been made successful by addicts for centuries, like cannabidiol (CBD), which has survived the test of time.

Naltrexone, Buprenorphine, and Narcan are new and effective opioid treatment medications, and these are having excellent success. However, synthetic opioids like Fentanyl and others, which are many time stronger than heroin, continue to kill many people from overdoses, mostly due to the intense craving that is inherent to opioid addiction.

Hopes are that hemp oil cannabidiol (CBD), which research has shown cuts craving—one of the most important culprits for addiction—will become a more widely used medication for the treatment of opioid addiction. It has been informally used by addicts in the streets for many decades, and its effectiveness has never failed. Hemp CBD offers hope and cure for the devastation that opioids is causing in the streets of America.

CHAPTER II

Ancient Remedies Used for Healing Addiction, and the Mysteries of CBD and Bear Bile

CHINESE MEDICINE IS considered to be one of the most ancient and most effective. Research has shown that the hemp plant, which contains cannabidiol (CBD), and other related plants were being used as medicine in China as far back as 4,000 BC for the treatment of addiction and other illnesses.

Much of Chinese medicine is based on the body being in balance. It is believed that the human body is made up of two opposites that must balance each other. These are the *yin* and the *yang*. If the person becomes ill, as in the case of an individual going through opioid withdrawals, then that person's body is out of balance. The use of herbs in healing illnesses of addiction to opioids is widely used in China with high levels of effectiveness, as it has for many centuries.[1]

Specifically, herbs are considered hot or cold based on their ability to cure illnesses. Cold is the yin, while hot is the yang. Examples of this medicinal concept are that:

1. Cold herbs (yin) treat the yang (hot) ailments such as inflammation and pains, as in opioid withdrawals

2. Hot herbs (yang) treat the yin (cold), as in the chills experienced in withdrawals and overdose.

In addition to the yin and the yang concept, Chinese medicine is of the belief that different flavors in herbs treat different ailments in the different organs of the body. Examples of these healing properties of flavors are as follows:

1. Spicy herbs speed up blood circulation, which is needed in treating overdose when the body starts shutting down and all vital signs start slowing down.

2. Salty herbs assist in bowel movements and cure constipation, typical in opioid addicts.

3. Bitter herbs produce heat, which will counter the chills of withdrawals.

4. Sweet herbs relieve pain, as in withdrawal pain.

5. Sour herbs stop sweating, coughing, and diarrhea, which occur in some opioid addicted individuals as they are detoxing.

In addition to the flavors concept in Chinese medicine, there are also the four main groups of herbal medicines that have been used since the beginning of time to treat many illnesses, including opioid addiction, which has been a problem in China for centuries. These four groups are as follows:

1. Monarch – These herbs target the immediate cause and symptom of the disease, such as infections, inflammation, and reduce fever. Some of the herbs in this category are the forsythia fruit and the honeysuckle flower.

2. Ministers – These herbs enhance the monarch's effects and also target the underlying symptoms. Some of these herbs are the burdock fruit, fermented soy beans, schizonepeta leaf, and the mint leaf. The hemp CBD plant has been used as a minister herb for many centuries in the Northern Hemisphere, in North, Central, and South America, especially among the indigenous population.

3. Assistants – Treat the secondary symptoms, eliminate toxins, and maximize the effects of the other herbs. Some of these herbs are red rhizome, bamboo leaf, and balloon flower.

4. Guides – These deliver the effects of the herbs to the target areas. Some of these herbs include the licorice root.

Herbal treatment of opioid addiction and other illnesses has been a long-standing tradition in the Chinese culture for many centuries. Usually a combination of herbs is used depending on the illness, the patient's age, gender, and body type. In Chinese culture it is believed that treatment following the four properties and five flavors promote the balance of the yin and yang, and this is followed by healing.

There are other ancient treatment techniques for opioid addiction that are gaining popularity in our American culture, and are revealing positive healing results. Some of these are:

1. Acupuncture – used to reduce pain and bring body into balance

2. Cupping – used as muscle therapy using suction to reduce pain and relieve anxiety

3. Fire therapy – used to open pores to get the body ready to accept herb-infused oil to heal pain and anxiety, experienced in the withdrawal stage of opioid addiction

4. Plant-burning technique – called *moxibustion*, used for pain and stress

5. CBD oil – derived from the hemp plant and used for pain, to relieve craving/anxiety, depression, and inflammation. This oil is also administered for stress, schizophrenic disorders, and seizures. Cannabidiol (CBD) is only one cannabinoid derived from a plant that contains over 100 different cannabinoids. It is felt that many secrets and mysteries exist within this complex plant that may very well open up and reveal many other cures. Presently, CBD has become a very

popular treatment/cure for many illnesses, including addiction.

In addition to the hemp plant CBD oil, the other treatment technique that holds much promise is the bear bile potion that has been used since the eighth century. The fact that a bear can go into hibernation and sleep for six months without eating or drinking water, and wakes up like he just slept for one night, has always been a mystery to experts that specialize in ancient medicine. Since the eighth century, Chinese people have used bear bile for liver problems, fever, and other ailments, with astonishing results. The unexplained mystery has raised many questions, such as:

1. How can a bear sleep for six months straight and show no ill effects, and can wake up at a moment's notice and fight any intruder who might want to invade his turf?

2. How can a 800-pound bear survive for six months only taking two breaths per minute and three pulses per minute without sustaining brain cell damage or suffer blood clotting due to extremely slow circulation?

3. How can a bear sleep for six months and lose only 50 percent of its body fat, but lose no muscle whatsoever?

4. There are many other questions too numerous for this primer.

Chinese doctors have studied these bear bile mysteries for many centuries, and they continue to do so. Presently, many doctors from many other countries have attempted to unravel these mysteries. Dr. Iaizzo, head of the University of Minnesota's Visible Heart Laboratory, has identified three bear bile components that trigger hibernation and that show much promise in the treatment of heart conditions and many other illnesses. These bile components are 1.) fatty acids, 2.) bile acids, and 3.) delta opioids. For the purpose of this writing, it is the contention that further study of the delta opioid component is merited as to how it can be used for the treatment of our present opioid epidemic.

As far-fetched as this may sound, bear bile and its delta opioid component hold a lot of promise, just like cannabidioil (CBD). Both have effectively been used for centuries by ancient medicine men and women, and it is felt that both contain medical secrets and mysteries that will help us solve this plaguing epidemic of opioid addiction. With over 90,000 deaths per year due to opioid overdoses, there is a tremendous need for innovative and creative research in the use of CBD, bear bile, and other out-of-the-box treatment techniques. And there is this great need to stop thinking that we are going to solve the opioid epidemic through incarceration. It is backfiring and openly not working.

It is felt that it might be as simple as the discovery of aspirin, when the ancient Egyptians discovered that myrtle leaves were good for relieving aches and pains. After that, in the fourth century, Hippocrates discovered that willow bark was good for fevers. Finally, in the 1800s, a European doctor discovered that both herbs contained salicylic acid, synthesized both of them, and came up with *aspirin*. The fact is, like the captain, CBD has already proven itself to be a great healer!

CHAPTER III

Cannabidiol (CBD) in the Beginning

CANNABIDIOL (CBD) FROM the hemp plant and from the cannabis plant has been used in China since 4,000 BC. Since the beginning, it was used for food, medicine, religious reasons, spiritual rituals, and for industrial fiber, as in rope making. Even the seeds of the hemp plant, which grow into a heart shape, have been used for thousands of years to treat heart and skin conditions. Apparently, these seeds are rich in omega-3. There is ample evidence that the Chinese people have been using opium for thousands of years and dealing with the addiction of the same. However, there is no record of Chinese individuals that suffered from addiction to hemp and/or cannabis. To the contrary, there is record of them using hemp and cannabis to treat people with opium addiction and other ailments.

Many years later, the new Spanish and English colonists in America grew hemp and cultivated it to use the plant's strong fibers to make rope, which at the time was widely used. There is also evidence that some of the colonists used part of the hemp plant to treat pain, anxiety, and even extracted its oil that was used as an elixir for many other ailments, and was one of the most popular so-called tonics of the day.

Since the late 1800s, it was very common along the southern border of the United States for home-grown herbologists to keep five-gallon jars with portions of the hemp and/or cannabis plants soaking in alcohol, ready to use for medicinal purposes. In addition to these soakers, there were always dried-up hemp and cannabis plants and other herbs that were used to make medicinal teas. The usual tea for pain contained hemp and mint. Most people did not know that what was reducing the pain was the cannabidiol (CBD) in the hemp, and that mint was basically an enhancer for the CBD. What they did know was that it reduced the pain, and that whatever chemicals were contained in those plants did the job of healing.

CBD use became very popular at the end of World War I and World War II. Many of the US soldiers returning from the wars returned addicted to morphine due to pain from their wounds. Not being able to afford the morphine medication and having many problems renewing their prescriptions, they quickly turned to street heroin. When the lack of heroin caused them pain, they quickly found that hemp oil and mint leaves eased their pain, of course not knowing at the time that it was the CBD doing the healing.

Understanding that the hemp CBD cannabinoid performed unexplained medical miracles, Professor Raphael Mechoulam from Hebrew University of Jerusalem, in 1963, began to perform modern-day research on CBD. It was in 1970 that Brazilian researchers revealed that CBD administered orally reduced anxiety and many of the symptoms in psychotic patients. Soon after all the mentioned research began, Sativex, a CBD-based medication, was produced by GW Pharmaceuticals out of the United Kingdom, and the use of this medication started worldwide for pain and spasticity (a sudden tightening of muscles creating pain), as well as other uses.

CHAPTER IV

Research-Based CBD Healing for Opioid Addiction and Other Illnesses

THERE IS AMPLE worldwide research that has been published on the effects of cannabidiol (CBD) that has revealed very positive medical treatment results for addiction and other illnesses.

Doctors Y. L. Hurd, M. Yoon, A. F. Manin, S. Hernandez, R. Olmedo, M. Ostman, and D. Jutras-Aswad published in the periodical *Neurotherapeutics* in October 12, 2015, their CBD research-based article entitled "Early Phase in the Development of Cannabidiol as a Treatment for Addiction: Opioid Relapse Takes Initial Center Stage," which revealed astonishing results. In summary, these researchers concluded that CBD is not addictive, thus having limited to no abuse potential at whatever dose that may be administered. Furthermore, they found that CBD inhibits drug-seeking behavior, which translates into virtually erasing one of the most critical phases of addiction, the *craving*, thus serving as a very effective therapeutic intervention for opioid relapse.

Another very interesting research project developed by Doctors F. S. Guimares, J. C. De Aguiar, R. Mechoulan, and A. Brewer, and published in the *Journal of General Pharmacology* in 1994, entitled "Anxiolytic Effect of Cannabidiol Derivatives in the Elevated Plus Maze," revealed very exact medically useful conclusions. These were that CBD has antipsychotic, antidepressant, and neuroprotective properties. These research findings contain endless positive and useful ramifications in the treatment of psychological, psychiatric, and addiction diagnosis.

A research project entitled "Cannabidiol: a Non-Psychotic Component of Cannabis Inhibits Cue-Induced Heroin Seeking and Normalizes Discrete Mesolimbic Neuronal Disturbance," published in the *Journal of Neuroscience* in 2009 by researchers Y. Ren, J. Whittard, A. Higuera-Mattas, C. V. Morris, and Y. L. Hurd reported some very interesting findings. These very important findings were that Cannabidiol (CBD) normalizes the heroin (opioid) induced changes in the CB1 receptor, MRNA expression, and AMPA GluR1 in the nucleus accumbens, even after two weeks of treatment. This suggests a long-term impact on neural mechanisms relevant to opioid relapse, which is a very important component in the treatment of opioid addicts. In simplified terms, CBD, when properly administered, *blocks cravings for opioids.*

It is appropriate at this point of this writing to provide some definitions in order to get the reader to better appreciate most research dealing with using CBD in the healing of addiction. Many addiction counselors define addiction in five stages. These five stages are:

I. Intoxication stage – is the stage when the drug produces what seem positive, euphoric, and rewarding experiences

II. Maintenance stage – is the stage when drug addiction is no longer about the high but of doing the drug to avoid the pain, anxiety, and stress of not having the drug in the human body

III. Withdrawal stage – is the stage when the user no longer has access to the drug (cold turkey) or is undergoing Detox, thus experiencing acute physical and psychological withdrawal symptoms if not properly medicated

IV. Relapse stage – is the stage when the addict has cold turkeyed or detoxed and is experiencing craving and is at risk of drug-seeking behavior and going back to doing the drugs

V. Recovery stage – is the stage where the addiction is recognized as a genetically predisposed illness, and where the addict must continually work at staying sober one day at a time by developing a strong support system and working the program; otherwise, the illness will win and the addict will fall back to the relapse stage

Once there is a basic understanding of the stages of addiction, one can better determine at every stage the services the addict will need, and the amount of CBD that can be used in the healing process that s/he must undergo. For example, there are ample studies that have concluded that CBD blocks craving; therefore, it is safe to assume that CBD works well in the relapse stage. Not only does it work well in the relapse stage but also in all the other stages, due to CBD being antianxiety/stress and also reducing pain.

Researchers have also concluded that CBD has proven to be very effective as a healing agent for many other illnesses other than addiction. The following are but a few examples of these.

A good example of this versatile healing is a study performed by researchers

T. V. Zanelate, C. Biojone, F. A. Moreira, F. S. Guimaraes, and S. R. Joca entitled "Anti-Depressant-like Effects of Cannabidiol in Mice: Possible Involvement of 5-HT1A Receptor" (*Journal of Pharmacology*, 2010), where it was clearly revealed that CBD has antidepressant and anticonvulsant effects. In a similar study, its anticonvulsive effects were very evident in epileptic patients. That study is entitled "Chronic Administration of Cannabidiol to Health Volunteers and Epileptic Patients," also published in the *Journal of Pharmacology* in 1980.

There has also been much concern regarding the side effects of cannabidiol (CBD). In relation to this, researchers

I. Tomida, A. Azuara-Blanco, H. House, M. Flint, R. G. Pertwee, and P. J. Robson performed a scientific study entitled "Effect of Sublingual Application of Cannabidiol on Intra-Ocular Pressure: A Pilot Study," where they found that CBD in various contexts reported no significant or serious adverse events other than mild sedation and nausea. This study was published in 2006 in the *Journal of Glaucoma*, and can also be found online under Public Medicine and Google Scholar.

In another related study, researchers Zuardian, S. L. Morais, F. S. Guimaraes, and R. Mechoulam clearly found that humans can tolerate daily cannabidiol (CBD) at high doses, as in psychotic patients. This study is entitled "Anti-Psychotic Effect on Cannabidiol." This study was published in 1995 in the *Journal of Clinical Psychiatry*.

Overall, researchers have determined that cannabidiol has anxiolytic, antipsychotic, and neuroprotective properties that assist in the healing process of epilepsy, substance abuse/dependence/comorbidities, schizophrenia, social phobia, PTSD, depression, bipolar disorder, sleep disorder, psychosis, anxiety disorder, and many other disorders. One example of this other research is that CBD has been found to regulate stress response and compulsive behavior, as common in the illness of addiction, as found by E. B. Russo, A. Burnett, B. Hall, and K. K. Parker in "Agonistic Properties of Cannabidiol at 5-HT1A Receptors," published in *Neurochemistry Research*.

Regarding the healing of addictions, CBD is an exogenous cannabinoid that acts on several neurotransmission systems involved in addiction, in particular in opioid addiction. Specific studies have shown that CBD inhibited the decrease of the intracranial self-stimulation (ICSS) threshold by morphine, and thus its reward-facilitating effect, without influencing motor function.

Even though CBD has been used for centuries in many cultures in the healing of addiction, it hasn't been until lately that researchers have determined why. Many of these whys have already been mentioned in prior text, but it all goes back to the healing medicines of the ancients, where it's all about CBD attaching itself to all healing body receptors and keeping the body in a stage of perfect equilibrium. Or as our ancient Asian ancestors called it, bringing the yin and the yang in perfect balance. Yes, society has come a long way from cure-All cannabidiol elixirs and hemp and cannabis plant particles soaking in alcohol, ready to be used as medicine, to science-based medicines like Sativex, EPIDIOLEX, and now Gummy Bears, drinks, droppers—and the list goes on and on!

Yes, there are many scientific studies that point toward the fact that CBD has many healing ingredients and that it has been very successful in the healing of opioid addiction, including addiction to synthetic opioids.

CHAPTER V

Being Genetically Predisposed to Addiction and Why Detox or Cold Turkey, and the Use of Hemp CBD

I T HAS TO be noted that addiction is an illness very much like diabetes and other illnesses. Researchers have concluded that it is a genetically predisposed disease. It is very interesting to see that in a family where every child has the same upbringing, two or three of the children will grow up to be strong and healthy and then one will end up being addicted. All these children went through the same developmental phases, where they drank, smoked cigarettes, and even experimented with marijuana, but then they left all that behind and moved on to become professionals. In the meantime, that one brother or sister got stuck in the drug world, and rather than smoking a little weed then moving up in life, that brother or sister went on to become a heroin addict, coke, methamphetamine, and/or synthetic opioid addict, when the others didn't. The saying goes that "not all that start with marijuana become addicts, but most addicts started with marijuana." Studies have been performed in these situations, and time and time again the addiction gene has been found in that one sibling and not the others.

The fact is that, that one person will carry the addiction gene all her/his life; therefore, she/he will always be predisposed to addiction. But that does not mean that, that person will be addicted all her/his life. It is very similar to the diabetic. Just because the person carries the diabetic gene, it does not mean that she/he will suffer from diabetes all her/his life. How many times have we seen the diabetic person exercise and diet and as a result stays healthy, and many times does not even need insulin. It's basically the same way with addiction. In other words, a person that is predisposed to addiction may choose to work her/his program daily and never become addicted. And if that person was once addicted, will never relapse again.

Working one's program may mean different things for different people, but seven important factors that have been found to be useful in living a drug-free lifestyle for the predisposed are as follows:

1. Join a support group like Alcoholics Anonymous, a PTSD group, a religious group, or any other group that will serve as your support system.

2. Choose your friends very carefully and avoid relationships that are high risk that might cause you to start using alcohol or drugs, or that might cause you to relapse.

3. Do not go to places where they serve alcohol and/or do drugs.

4. Join a spiritual group where you can get in touch with your higher power.

5. Unless it is totally dysfunctional, choose family first and get and give support from those who love you.

6. Choose a physical activity that you can participate in daily.

7. Choose a partner that shares your views on life, and do not deviate from your program for any reason.

However, if you and/or your loved one are already using synthetic opioids, heroin, and/or other opioids, think detox or cold turkey (kicking the habit on your own) and act on it. Rest assured, if you continue using, you will eventually overdose if you are going to start chipping (doing a little bit because you just know you will not get addicted again). You need to know that when you overdose, what happens is that the opioid drug is so strong that it slows down all your vital organs until they completely shut down and you die. The chances of that happening to you are very high and inevitable if you continue using. Therefore, as you await your upcoming overdose, go to the nearest drug store and buy a small spray can of NARCAN, which may be used to revive people as they are overdosing from opioids. Read the instructions when you are not under the influence and remember them so that you might save your friend's life or vice versa.

If you are lucky to survive your first overdose, you will probably not survive the next one. You seem to get weaker at every overdose. In view of this, and if you really want to save your life, go into a detox program or cold turkey yourself. A detox program is preferable, because experience states that many cold turkey, self-detox attempts usually end up in an overdose because most addicts attempt to taper down. And this might work, until you run into a batch of opioids that might be 100 times stronger than what your body is used to, and you overdose and die. It is very common to hear on TV about twenty-some people overdosing in the same small town on the same day, because they use heroin laced or mixed with the synthetic drug Fentanyl, which is many times stronger than street heroin. In other words, as strong as you might be, your body will not be able to handle it and you'll overdose.

If you do not know of a drug detox program, then Google it or simply call your local health department or the fire station closest to you. These offices always know where you can go. If you cannot afford the detox costs, then look for a locally, state, or federally funded program. There is always one available. These programs are free of charge. Or go to www. samhsa.gov.

As you are withdrawing from the opioids, you will feel anxiety, pain, and general discomfort. If you are cold turkeying by yourself, you might want to consider taking cannabidiol (CBD) to relieve your pain, anxiety, and general discomfort. This CBD Oil can be found in most drug Stores. If you are detoxing under the direction of a doctor, do not take CBD unless the doctor gives authorization. Many doctors nowadays choose CBD rather than synthetic medications due to the fact that CBD has no side effects and is not habit forming.

Research has shown that CBD provides healing for all the stages of addiction, including the maintenance stage, when the addict is under a lot of pain and desperate not to get sicker due to the lack of the drug. It has also proven to be quite helpful during withdrawal, as in detox or cold turkey stage, which translates to the addict cleansing his system of the drug and undergoing a physical reaction as a result of the absence of the drug. At this stage, CBD assists in reducing pain and anxiety. Much research has also been performed about the use of CBD in the relapse stage, and as mentioned in prior text, CBD has been shown to block the craving, which is so evident during this stage.

In total, CBD research has shown that CBD contains antipsychotic, antidepressant, neuroprotective, and anxiolytic properties useful in the healing of not only opioid addiction, but also addiction to methamphetamines and cocaine, in addition to modulating opioid receptors in the brain. Other than healing addictions, CBD has proven effective in the healing of epilepsy, sleep disorders, schizophrenia, anxiety disorders, and many other illnesses.

CHAPTER VI

Solving the Drug Epidemic by Transitioning from Incarceration to a Responsibly Funded, Natural (CBD), Innovative, and Creative Drug Treatment System

O UR GREAT UNITED States of America is the land of innovation and the free, and it is becoming the land of the most incarceration. In a large part, it has become this way because sometime in the 1980s America decided it was going to treat the illness of addiction through incarceration. In doing so, according to the Bureau of Justice statistics, America went from having approximately 500,000 people behind bars in 1980 to over 2,000,000 presently. Matter of fact, according to the World Prison Brief, America has more people behind bars than Russia, China, Japan, and the Netherlands put together.

According to the Department of Justice (DOJ) statistics, approximately 80 percent of inmates are in prison due to drug addiction and/or drug-related offenses. Furthermore, according to the latest *Federal Register*, the cost per inmate is approximately $100 per day, which translates to America spending approximately $200 million per day on incarceration. As can be noted, mass incarceration is a two-edged sword. It is big business, creating jobs, with private companies' participation, and at the same time it is an embarrassment to America on the international stage to have the most people in prison in comparison to all other nations. All this translates to one thing, and this is that America will never solve drug illness through mass incarceration.

If America is going to be successful in seriously addressing its drug addiction epidemic, than it must finally accept that addiction is an illness and treat it as such. After all, research has proven many times over that treatment works with addicted sick people. Even though it works, it has not received the needed attention and funding required to develop viable addiction treatment that is an on-demand and as-needed system at all levels. For over forty years, we have operated an ill-funded and crippled drug services system at all levels.

The following are some serious, new, and innovative fiscal strategies that are needed to produce enough funding for the development and implementation of best practice and science-based programming that will turn this horrendous drug epidemic around. These strategies are as follows:

1. Implement a twenty-hour drug education/prevention and parenting course for couples applying for a marriage license, followed by a drug test at the end of the course. An additional fee of $200 must be paid by each couple. All positive drug tests will be denied a license and will

be referred to drug abuse services. After undergoing drug services and producing a negative drug test result, the couple will become eligible again to apply for their marriage license. The money generated by the entity issuing marriage licenses must reinvest it in drug services programming. Furthermore, all couples applying for a divorce must also pay another $200 drug prevention/education fee that will be spent on drug prevention services for children. In essence, this fee will generate some funding, and at the same time teach new parents how to deal with their drug issues and their children.

2. All pharmaceutical companies producing and/or distributing medications that are natural- and/or synthetic-based opioids, barbiturates, amphetamines, and/or related medication must pay a 10 percent drug treatment, prevention, education, intervention, and recovery fee to the federal drug services entity known as the Substance Abuse and Mental Health Services Administration (SAMHSA). SAMHSA will distribute the money collected from this fee nationally through their existing proposal system.

3. Fifty percent of all assets of all forfeitures, restitutions, and confiscations in all drug and/or drug-related cases must be invested in drug treatment, intervention, prevention, education, and recovery programming, and deposited to the SAMHSA account, which will

in turn distribute the money nationally through its proposal system.

4. All marijuana and hemp growers, wholesalers, and retailers must pay a 10 percent revenue fee, which will also be credited to the SAMHSA federal account that will also be used as above mentioned.

5. All vaping and e-cigarette wholesalers and retailers must all pay a 10 percent revenue fee that will also be invested as above mentioned.

6. All private correctional companies profiting from the drug epidemic incarceration strategy must also pay a 10 percent revenue fee that will also be invested as above mentioned.

7. All wine, beer, and hard liquor wholesalers and retailers must also pay a 10 percent drug services revenue fee, which will also be invested as above mentioned.

8. All existing federal general revenue budget amounts being presently allocated and invested on drug services through formula and categorical and other federal funding mechanisms must be increased by a minimum of 20 percent, in that America is fighting a drug addiction epidemic that has grown into a national health emergency.

9. All medications that are being imported from other countries must also pay a 20 percent fee before they

enter America, and this fee will also be invested as above mentioned.

It is the opinion of this writer that the above innovative, creative, and responsible funding plan will generate enough resources to finally launch a realistic effort to solve the growing and devastating drug epidemic. Presently, many addicts are being left untreated because there is simply not enough money to do it!

Most of the treatment that is being administered in America is working; however, the resources are not reaching all those in need, and that is the problem. In the first place, a very low percentage of those needing treatment are actually in treatment due to there not being enough funds. The need at the present time is that every American that is addicted or close to becoming addicted should be in treatment. Also, every young American at the primary/high school level needs to undergo a drug education and prevention class. There is also a great need for intervention, recovery, and of course the therapeutic potential of natural healing remedies like CBD and other proven best practice remedies.

Upon looking at a fifty-year history of drug-abuse services in America at different levels, the below are some of the needs for the existing system that are working well, but the fact remains that they are just not enough. Some of these needs are as follows:

1. Excellent addiction research is being performed by the National Institute of Drug Abuse (NIDA) but more

is needed, especially in the area of neurocircuitry and the specific genetics of addiction and the effects of natural healing remedies like CBD and other ancient and natural medicines, and their effects at every stage of addiction. A 20 percent increase in NIDA's budget is desperately needed in that for years the NIDA budget has been very limited in comparison to the need.

2. Again, excellent work is also being performed by the Substance Abuse and Mental Health Services Administration (SAMHSA) and the different state drug services offices across the country. However, again, these offices are very budget restricted; thus, only reaching a very limited number of addicts in need. This is why it is being recommended that the prior mentioned revenue fee go to SAMHSA, plus a 20 percent general federal budget increase. SAMHSA counts many years of experience in managing drug services grants. Therefore, having done this in excellent fashion for many years, SAMHSA should lead in this new funding distribution.

3. It has been said many times that the best treatment for all addicts is a sustainable job, and this is very true. In view of this, 20 percent of the revenue fees collected should be earmarked for the Department of Labor and the Department of Education. These agencies will work in coordination with all drug services agencies and state and federal prisons to ensure that every addict that has undergone treatment will immediately

transition to sustainable employment on day one after treatment or upon release from prison.

4. That all drug service agencies be encouraged to use the latest science-based medications and nonaddictive best practice natural healing remedies in every stage of treatment. Some of these healing remedies are CBD, bear bile, acupuncture, pressure pointing, ancient body balancing, herbal formulas, hypnosis, physical therapy, moxibustion treatment (plant burning), herbal bathing, alcohol fire treatment, spiritual therapy, music therapy, nutrition therapy, and many other innovative treatment techniques that are not addictive.

5. Develop and immediately operationalize an intensive community outreach effort in every community in America led by teams of paraprofessional ex-addicts that will seek out all opioid addicts and provide the following services:

   A. Convince, recruit, and transport all addicts into treatment

   B. Assist the family, while the addict is in treatment, in obtaining food, medical care transportation, and any other need the family might have

   C. Work with the Department of Labor (DOL), local workforce solution offices, and the IRS in obtaining sustainable employment or vocational training for all addicts upon release from treatment or prison

D. Provide intensive antirelapse aftercare to every addict at all social levels and their family, and act quickly at the first sign of possible relapse

6. Revise and upgrade the national controlled substance registry as follows:

A. Adding more internal auditors, whose job should be reconciling on a daily basis all amounts of controlled medications being produced by pharmaceutical corporation or being imported by wholesalers/retailers with the prescriptions being issued by doctors and prescriptions being filled by patients at local pharmacies

B. Establishing a compliance task force that, at a moment's notice, can be activated and travel to the entity that is showing irregularities and enforce the law immediately on the spot

C. All entities out of compliance with the law must pay noncompliance fees or forfeiture, restitution, and/or confiscation fees after they have undergone due process. Again, all funds generated at this point will be deposited to the SAMHSA account, which will in turn fund drug service efforts across the country.

Again, these above noted are simply recommendations based on four decades of frontline experience and study. The current laws are not being considered as these recommendations are being made. The goal here is to provide recommendations that will provide the funding and new and improved efforts to finally take control of the drug epidemic that is rampant throughout America, with special emphasis in taking treatment to every home in need instead of waiting for the opioid addict to come on their own.

CHAPTER VII

Hemp Cannabidiol (CBD): The Hottest Healing Remedy on the Market Today

WHAT EXACTLY IS hemp cannabidiol (CBD) and why is it the hottest and most popular healing remedy on the market at the present time? Why are people all over the world all of a sudden claiming that CBD contains many health boosting and healing qualities?

Hemp CBD oil is derived from the hemp plant, and this plant has been used in America and around the world for many years to make rope and other products that require strong fiber. Also, for many years grandmothers have been soaking it in alcohol and using it as a pain remedy for sprained joints, pulled muscles, headaches, and so on. Presently, after so many years, Americans are crazy about CBD oil, and the claims are that this oil, even though there is need for more research, is a healing remedy for the decrease of pain, improving sleep, reducing stress, calming the nervous system, reducing inflammation; that it is neuroprotective, reduces anxiety, reduces PTSD episodes, reduces seizure disorders (epilepsy), reduces schizophrenic episodes; that it modulates endorphins, also modulates our immune system (fibromyalgia, chronic fatigue syndrome, and chronic bowel diseases, Chron's disease, ulcerative colitis), anti-tumor, antioxidant, antimicrobial, and heals a variety of heart conditions through its heart-shaped seeds that contain vast amounts of omega-3 and that it heals different addictions.

In order to better understand CBD oil, we must first address the extraction methods that are used to take the oil out of the hemp plant. There are four main extraction methods, and these are as follows:

1. CO_2 extraction – Carbon dioxide is used to extract the chemical components from the flower buds of the plant, then distilled into a dense CBD oil.

2. Chemical extraction – This extraction method uses alcohol and hexane to produce the oil.

3. Lipid-based extraction – Uses fats such as coconut oil to absorb and incapsulate the plant compounds, thus making CBD oil easy to absorb; however, this method does not produce the most medicinal full-spectrum CDB oil.

4. Vapor distillation extraction – Also known as thermal extraction because it uses hot oil to safely vaporize the more medicinal full-spectrum oil from the flower buds, then the vapor is distilled into CBD oil. This method activates all the existing cannabinoids (decarboxylation), which produces what is called full-spectrum CBD or full-value CBD, because in addition

to extracting the CBD oil it also preserves the terpene component, which in itself is also a strong healing and enhancing extract.

After extraction, CBD is converted into five different types of oils. These are as follows:

1. Full-spectrum CBD oil is the type that provides a full range of chemical components, including the medicinal terpenes. This type of CBD oil is the most expensive, and claims are that it is the most medicinal.

2. Purified CBD, this oil only contains CBD.

3. Broad-spectrum CBD oil is the full-spectrum oil without the terpenes.

4. Isolate CBD oil, also only contains CBD without any of the other components.

5. The entourage effect CBD is the full spectrum but elevated in the other components and strength.

Now that the extraction and conversion methods have been explained, how is CBD oil administered and/or used? There are also five ways to medicinally use CBD oil. These are as follows:

1. Sublingual – This is the best way to use CBD oil because it is the most direct and the fastest acting. Using a dropper, you simply apply the drops of the prescribed amount under the tongue and allow it to

stay there for a couple of minutes, and the membranes under the tongue will do all the work of directly absorbing the oil.

2. Mouth and swish – This is the method where, again using a dropper or drinking a CBD drink, you swish it around your mouth, then swallow it, thus allowing all the membranes in your mouth and stomach to do the absorption.

3. Vaping – This is the method that is widely used by the younger generation, where a CBD e-liquid is smoked, but it's also the most controversial at this time.

4. Soft gel capsules – This method is widely used, even though some of the effects are diluted in the stomach and intestines.

5. Other methods of administration – These include the edibles (cookies, Gummy Bears, soups, etc.), drinks, aromas, etc.

It must be explained at this time that hemp CBD does not produce a high at whatever dosage and/or form of administration, simply because it does not contain the psychoactive drug that will produce the high. Research shows that it is nonaddictive ("Translational Investigation of the Therapeutic Potential of Cannabidiol (CBD): Toward a New Age in Frontiers in Immunology" by researchers J. A. Crippa, F. S. Guimaraes, A. C. Campos, and A. W. Zuardi, online, 2018).

CBD oil is packaged in different strengths, and one must be careful to make sure that one is taking the prescribed amount that the clinician orders. Just to make sure, one must take into consideration absorption rate, CBD oil type, dilution due to form of administration, and so on.

The following sample table may be used to provide some direction when taking CBD oil.[9]

SAMPLE DOSAGE TABLE

<u>1 fluid oz. bottle of</u>		<u>1 dropperful equivalent</u>
100 mgs of CBD oil	=	3.3 mgs of CBD oil
250 mgs of CBD oil	=	8.3 mgs of CBD oil
500 mgs of CBD oil	=	16.7 mgs of CBD oil
600 mgs of CBD oil	=	20.0 mgs of CBD oil
800 mgs of CBD oil	=	26.7 mgs of CBD oil
1,000 mgs of CBD oil	=	33.3 mgs of CBD oil
1,500 mgs of CBD oil	=	50.0 mgs of CBD oil

In reference to CBD edibles (cookies, Gummy Bears, etc.), capsules, and drinks, the strength of the CBD is usually marked on the package. And if it isn't, you might want to ask. Even though they are marked, take into consideration absorption and dilution rates depending on the form of administration. Always follow the orders of the clinician.

There is still some debate and research being performed as to the proper CBD dosage for the different ailments. Do consult with your clinician to determine the proper CBD dosage for your specific condition. Even though the US Federal Drug Administration (FDA) has not fully endorsed CBD dosages, the following are a few research-based dosages that have been concluded as the result of research being performed:[9]

1. 5 mgs per day for three days of full-spectrum CBD – Research has concluded that it has specifically inhibited conditioned cue-induced heroin-seeking behavior ("CBD Influences the Relapse Phase of Opioid Addiction by Decreasing Cue-Induced Drug Seeking Behaviors" by researchers: Y. Ren, J. W. Whittard, A. Higuearra-Mattas, C. V. Morris, and J. L. Hurd, published in the *Journal of Neurosciences*)

2. 300 to 600 mgs per day of full-spectrum CBD – Research has concluded that this dosage has antidepressant and anticonvulsive effects as per research entitled "Chronic Administration of Cannabidiol to Health Volunteers and Epileptic Patients" by researchers J. M. Cunha, E. A. Carlini, A. E. Pereira, et al., published in the *Journal of Pharmacology*

3. In another research study entitled "Cannabidiol as an Intervention for Addictive Behaviors: A Systematic Review of the Evidence" published by researchers M. Prudhomme, R. Cata, and D. Jutras-Aswad, it was revealed that CBD has therapeutic properties in the treatment of opioids, cocaine, and psychostimulant addiction. This research was published in Canada at the research center Centre Hospitalier de Universite

4. 300 mgs of CBD has proven to be effective in healing anxiety as shown in a research study entitled "Effects of Isapirone and Cannabidiol on Human's Experimental Anxiety" by researchers A. W. Zuardi, R. A. Cosme,

F. G. Graeff, and F. S. Guimaraes, and published in *Journal of Psychopharmacology*

5. 1,280 mgs of CBD per day for thirty days administered to acute schizophrenia patients revealed marked improvement according to a research study entitled "Cannabidiol Monotherapy for Treatment Resistant Schizophrenia" published by researchers A. W. Zuardi, J. E. Hallak, and S. M. Musty in the *Journal of Psychopharmacology*

6. A very interesting research study by researchers G. F. Koob and N. D. Volkow entitled "A Widely Used Conceptualization of Addiction Looks at CBD Effects on Intoxication, Withdrawal and Relapse (Craving)," published in the *Journal of Neurocircuitry of Addiction and Neuropsychopharmacology* in 2010, is futuristic and contains a wealth of information for those interested in the field of addiction.

7. 50 mgs per day of CBD for two weeks exercises its effects via several neural mechanisms relevant to addictive disorders. It normalizes the heroin-induced changes even after two weeks of treatment, as revealed in the research study entitled "Cannabidiol: A Non-Psychotropic Component Inhibits Cue-Induced Heroin Seeking and Normalizes Discrete Mesolimbic Neuronal Disturbances" by researchers Y. Ren, J. Whittlard, A. Higuerra Mattas, C. V. Morris, and J. L. Hurd. This study was published in the *Journal of Neurosciences.*

There is more research that has been published regarding CBD, but the above cases were selected to simply illustrate that there is some validity to some of the present healing claims. However, much more research is needed in the field. This writing only begins to explain why CBD is so hot as a healing oil at this time, and why many people swear that it heals when nothing else has been able to!

And lastly, the Mayo Clinic has also made the following dosage recommendations:

a.) Loss of appetite (cancer patients): 1 mg of CBD daily for six weeks

b.) Chronic pain: 2.5 to 20 mg of CBD per day orally

c.) Epilepsy: 200–300 mgs of CBD orally daily

d.) Sleep disorders: 40–160 mgs of CBD orally daily

e.) Schizophrenia: 280 mgs CBD orally daily

f.) Glaucoma: single sublingual CBD dose of 20–40 mgs daily

The above are simply recommendations, and consultation with your doctor is recommended before considering these dosages in that s/he would have to take your medical history and status into consideration.

CHAPTER VIII

HB 1325[35] Regulating Hemp, Cannabidiol (CBD), and Other By-Products of Same

IN 2018, THE president of the United States signed the Federal Farm Bill legalizing hemp nationally and setting law regulating the plant. Even though this law authorized the states to proceed according to the law, Texas enacted its own hemp legalization statute, House Bill 1325, in June of 2019. Both the federal law and the Texas law contain basically the same provisions, and the following is a general summary of the Texas law governing hemp. This summary is as follows:

1. That the State Health and Human Services Commission (HHSC) in coordination with the Federal Department of Agriculture (DOA) will develop procedures and implement the law, while the Texas Department of Public Safety (DPS) will regulate and enforce the law.

2. All hemp and by-products transported in the State of Texas must have in their possession a shipping certificate and a cargo manifest, and the shipment must meet all Department of Agriculture (DOA) laws.

3. No hemp and/or by-products can be shipped along with other products in the same cargo, and no hemp cargo can contain plant diseases and/or signs of pesticides. And the DPS and/or any other law enforcement officer may seize the cargo for probable cause, make an arrest if the cargo does not have the proper documentation and/or may be mixed with marijuana.

4. Civil action can be brought against any transporter and company for any shipment/cargo violation for the amount of $500 for each violation or $1,000 for enforcement penalties, and administrative penalties may also be imposed.

5. A hemp-growing license is required from the Federal Department of Agriculture (DOA) and any violation of the enhanced testing procedure will result in a $500 penalty.

6. Three violations within a five-year period by a grower, transporter, wholesaler, or retailer will cause that person or business entity to be placed on a banned list, where the person and/or business entity will not be allowed to work and/or operate a hemp business from that point on.

7. All "culpable mental state greater than negligence" will be referred to the attorney general and DPS for investigation and to institute proceedings or take injunctive action.

8. All manufacturing, distribution, and sale of consumable hemp products (food, drugs, devices, cosmetics, etc.) containing one or more hemp-derived cannabinoids, including CBD, as regulated by the State Department of Health (SDOH), requires an annual license issued by the State Department of Health for a fee, and the same department must enforce all rules of Chapter 443.101 of the law. The license application includes legal description of each location, where hemp will be manufactured, and the global positioning system coordinates for the perimeter of each location. The application shall also contain a written consent for the Department. of Public Safety (DPS) and/or any other law enforcement agency to enter the premise at any time.

9. All consumable hemp products shall be tested in accordance to subchapter D, Section A443.151 for concentration of cannabinoids, heavy metals, pesticides, microorganisms, residual solvents, and THC concentrations that, according to law, should not be more than -0.3 percent. This testing must be performed in accordance to the International Organization for Standardization (ISO) 17025. A copy of these test results must be submitted to all retailers selling hemp products to the public. Hemp State Law HB 1325 also regulates nonconsumable hemp products such as cloth, cordage, fiber, fuel, paint, paper, particle board, and plastics.

10. No retailer at any time can sell any cannabidiol (CBD) in the State of Texas that has been derived from the plant *Cannabis sativa* L. All CBD must be derived from the hemp plant and produced in compliance with 7 USC Chapter 38, Sub-Chapter VII.

11. A hemp grower's license is required according to Chapter 122 of HB 1325 Hemp Law for any individual or business that cultivates, plants, irrigates, or harvests hemp, including possessing or storing it (Section A 122.101). No individual with a felony history will be allowed a license for a period of ten years.

12. The State Department of Health will establish a hemp production account and will have the authority to charge the following fees: initial license = $100; renewal = $100; site modification = $500; testing fee $300 (organic certification required). And the Department of Public Safety (DPS) will also charge a participation fee, and will perform random inspections. All permits, licenses, and manifests will be checked by the law enforcement communication system and operated by DPS.

13. DPS will perform random CBD testing at any facility and/or store, including all retailers handling CBD. There is a one-year registration fee that must be paid, and DPS will test to assure that no CBD products contain more than 0.3 percent THC and that there is no harmful ingredient in the product. All irregular test

results (Section A443.203) will be processed as per the deceptive trade practice statutes of state law.

14. According to the hemp HB 1325 state law, CBD is not considered a controlled substance, and smokeable CBD is prohibited. This state law does not legalize marijuana in any shape or form.

15. According to Section 443.205 of this hemp state law, packaging and labeling of CBD products must contain the following: a.) batch ID number; b.) batch date; c.) product name; d.) uniform resource locator; e.) certification that Delta 9 links to a certificate of analysis stipulating a -0.3 percent THC result; f.) QR code; g.) label must appear on each unit, inside and outside. (This section does not apply to sterilized seeds incapable of germinating.)

16. CBD produced in other states may be used in Texas as long as it is approved by the Federal Department of Agriculture (DOA). Furthermore, transporting and exporting of consumable hemp products out of state (Section 443.2017) is permitted under federal law.

The above sixteen summary points describing the hemp law in Texas are not all inclusive; however, they are considered the most important.

CHAPTER IX

Opioid Epidemic Profiteering: CBD Part of the Answer

CBD MIGHT VERY well become a major part of the answer to the solution to the opioid addiction epidemic in America. Research has clearly concluded that CBD inhibits conditioned cue-induced opioid-seeking behavior. In other words, CBD blocks the "craving" that drives opioid addicts to continuously seek opioid drugs regardless of the consequences ("CBD Influences the Relapse Phase of Opioid Addiction by Decreasing Cue-Induced Drug Seeking Behaviors" by researchers Y. Ren, C. V. Morris, J. W. Whittard, A. Higuerra-Mattas, and J. L. Hurd).

According to the data of the DEA's Automation of Reports and Consolidated Orders System (ARCOS), the Drug Enforcement Administration (DEA) reported that from 2006 to 2012 America was saturated with an astonishing 76 billion prescription opioid pill—about 230 for every adult and child in the country (*El Paso Times Newspaper*, August 14, 2019).

ARCOS also has concluded that in 2020 approximately 90,000 Americans died of opioid overdose, which is an astonishing increase from approximately 8,000 in 1999. Even though this is happening in our country, the production and distribution of these deadly pain killers keep rising. Again, CBD may very well become a major part of the answer to this devastating dilemma, because not only will it cut the "craving" for opioids, but it also is a remedy for the reduction of pain without getting people addicted. CBD also reduces anxiety, which is very common in opioid withdrawal. An example of this is the well-known CBD medication known as "Sativex" developed by GW in the United Kingdom, which is used worldwide for pain, anxiety, and spasticity, as in multiple sclerosis. The sad part about this horrendous epidemic is that these devastating opioid pain killers continue killing Americans by the thousands, yet they are continuously produced in scandalous numbers.

At last Americans are fighting back against these unscrupulous profiteers. Very recently, the State of Oklahoma sued a pharmaceutical company and its subsidiary for billions of dollars for creating havoc, damages, shattering lives, and the loss of lives in the thousands in their state by producing and distributing synthetic opioids in their state. Our best sources at this time have revealed that the courts have awarded the State of Oklahoma considerably less than they were requesting, receiving a bit over $500 million. This in the minds of many is a step in the right direction. Even though the company and its subsidiary are expected to appeal the decision, the Oklahoma State Commissioner of Mental Health and Drug Abuse is already making plans to spend this money on the provision of drug education, treatment, prevention, and recovery for those Oklahomans plagued with the sickness of opioid addiction.

Another example of Americans fighting back is that the company who introduced the opioid medication OxyContin in the mid-1990s is in the process of settling a federal lawsuit with the government for over four billion dollars. In addition to the mentioned, another pharmaceutical company has settled another lawsuit for $85 million, and this company had already settled another lawsuit in 2007 for approximately $634 million. America is fighting back, with those who have lost family members taking the lead.

Furthermore, according to the DEAs' ARCOS data system, between the years 2006 and 2012, over 60 billion pills were produced by several major pharmaceutical companies. In addition to the producers, there are several major chains that are distributing these synthetic opioids in large numbers. This distribution by drugstores usually starts very innocently as a result of perhaps injury pain, but many times in the process this results in synthetic opioid addiction, and at times, unfortunately, in overdose death.

It is a well-known fact that treatment works; however, it always boils down to needing enough funding to reach all those in need. A new and innovative funding formula needs to be developed nationally. One that makes all responsible groups provide some of this needed funding.

The following are some ideas that need to be considered in seriously addressing this opioid epidemic:

1. That every business producing synthetic opioids, distributing, wholesaling, and/or retailing these addictive pain killers and killers of people must pay a 10 percent gross revenue fee that will go to the federal government office in charge of drug education, prevention, research, treatment, and recovery to be used for services, and 50 percent of the fee will go to the DEA for enforcement.

2. That the DEA's ARCOS data system be revised to include a digital programming component that will alert the DEA enforcement unit when there are irregularities, and immediately activate an official investigation. Any minor infraction will be penalized financially and referred to the US attorney's office for adjudication and prosecution.

Refer to Chapter VI, "Solving the Drug Epidemic by Transitioning from Incarceration to a Responsibly Funded Natural (CBD), Innovative, and Creative Drug Treatment System," for further recommendations.

Many companies producing and distributing these life-taking pills claim that they were simply taking orders. The fact is that they failed to report exorbitant amounts of orders.

Let's face it, evidence has been presented and will continue to come up where drug makers, wholesalers, retailers, and doctors committed grave errors.

It is very clear that from all this synthetic opioid death tragedy we are learning many lessons. One of the hardest lessons is that powerful synthetic pain medication kills more than it helps.

In view of this, America must search for natural nonaddictive pain medicine like CBD and other natural plant remedies and solutions. Research seems to indicate that cannabidiol (CBD) blocks pain-conducting nerve impulses, which reduces the perception of pain (Dr. Bill Rawls, *The Science Behind CBD*). In addition, CBD increases natural endorphins, which naturally suppress pain. Contrary to synthetic opioids, CBD relieves pain without causing a "drug high," intoxication, and/or addiction. Herbal and alternative medicine like CBD is believed to be part of the solution to the horrendous synthetic opioid epidemic. We need to stop synthetic opioids from killing our people, and we need to do it NOW!

Lastly, the *El Paso Times* newspaper reported (October 22, 2019) another victory in that two counties in Ohio settled a series of opioid lawsuits for $260 million from several drug makers. Several other claims were left unsettled in the same case. The victorious counties plan on investing the settlement monies in recovery programs.

All these settlements are sending a very loud message to synthetic drug makers, which will hopefully help in turning this epidemic around, that the drugs that heal end up killing.

Lastly, an important recommendation is that every doctor prescribing high doses of synthetic pain killers must order the patient to also undergo an addiction class that will be monitored by the DEA.

CHAPTER X

Step by Step: Caring for a Family Member That Is Addicted

MANY FAMILIES IN America go through a lot of pain, loss of life, and sustain much financial loss in their attempts to care for addicted sons, daughters, husbands, wives, grandsons, granddaughters, and so on. Some of these families get so desperate that they go as far as selling the equity to their home mortgages to obtain money to pay for treatment of their loved ones, when in reality the loved one is not ready and might be simply manipulating the family's love.

In many instances the addict goes in and out of treatment, which creates a "revolving door" circuit, or simply tells the family that s/he is all right now and that they do not need the treatment. The message here is if the addict is not ready, it does not matter how many times s/he is admitted into treatment, it is not going to work. Why, because it is a sickness in which regardless of the pain and consequences the craving is very intense, thus totally dominating the life of the addict. So intense that an addict will go to great lengths and do horrendous things for the next fix. Some addicts go as far as selling their cars and savings to quench that craving. If the time is not right, all the treatment in the world will not work. If the time is not right, sometimes an intervention by an experienced ex-addict might be able to put sense into the individual that s/he has no other options, and explain that s/he knows what s/he is talking about because s/he has been there. The question remains, when is it the right time for treatment?

The following thirteen steps to caring for an addicted family member are based on over five decades of experience working with addicts, and experiencing addiction firsthand and personally. These steps have been written by family members who have learned by their own experiences, and are lessons that have been taught and learned. In essence, these steps are considered "best practice." The hopes and goals of the following steps are to answer as clearly and directly as possible the many questions that families have when dealing with an addicted family member. These steps are as follows:

STEP I: Never allow illegal drugs or the use of drugs in your home. And if they are prescribed, monitor their use closely. Never allow the use of alcohol by minors in your home, even at parties. Enforce a zero-tolerance rule at all times.

STEP II: Lock up all prescribed opioids and other habit-forming drugs in your home and at the other homes of relatives, especially grandparents. Enforce a zero-access rule at all times.

STEP III: Never give or lend money to a family member that is addicted, and notify other family members to do the same in that you can be assured that this money will be used to buy drugs.

STEP IV: Buy cans of NARCAN (opioid overdose nasal spray) and learn how to use it, just in case your family member overdoses in front of you. Also buy another can of NARCAN for the relatives of your addicted family member's best friend who might be addicted also, and show them how to use the spray can to bring back addicts who have passed out as a result of an overdose, thus saving the life of that particular addict.

STEP V: Never bail out of jail an addicted family member, even though it will hurt you not to do so. The longer the addict is in jail, the longer s/he is going to be drug free, and the better it is for her/him and for the entire family.

STEP VI: Secure all valuables at home, especially those that may be sold or pawned, because eventually the addicted family member will steal from you and/or other family members (grandparents are prime targets).

STEP VII: Never, ever pick up an addicted family member that is living on the streets and give her/him a ride, because more than likely you might be used as a mule without you knowing. There are countless stories of this type of situation, where the addicted family member manipulates a mother to take her/him to buy drugs or deliver drugs. And oftentimes both get arrested, when in reality the mother knew nothing about the drug deal.

STEP VIII: Ban the addicted family member from home, as hard as it might be, and advise the extended family members to do the same. Not doing so translates into having valuable items and/or money being stolen to support the drug habit, or converting your home into a drug stash house. Admit her/him back once they've undergone treatment and have been drug free for several months or if a licensed drug counselor recommends it, but accept this with reservations.

STEP IX: Make yourself and your family strong and don't enable or support a family member who is actively addicted to opioids or any other drug. Do not allow yourself or your family to be used by the addicted family member as s/he starts asking for favors.

STEP X: Do not force any family member who is addicted to go into treatment. Most often it will be a waste of money and effort. The addict has to do it by herself/himself, and for herself/himself and not for anybody else.

STEP XI: Learn the stages of addiction and acquire the ability to recognize each one. These are 1.) intoxication stage, 2.) maintenance stage, 3.) withdrawal stage, 4.) relapse stage, and 5.) recovery stage. Refer to Chapter IV of this primer for a summary explanation of each one of these stages. This type of knowledge is essential for the family in order to understand the addicted family member.

STEP XII: Allow the addicted family member to "hit rock bottom," at which time s/he will seek drug treatment themselves. This is the perfect time for the family to seek assistance from ex-addict counselors who have gone through the sickness of addiction and all the stages themselves. The treatment success rate seems to be very high with addicts reaching this step.

STEP XIII: Once the addicted family member has been successful in her/his treatment, allow her/him to return home on a probationary basis. Do not shower her/him with gifts and money, and most of all, do not over love her/him. This enabling might cause a relapse, and then the cycle, unfortunately, starts all over again. The recommendation at this time is to give her/him a lot of tough love!

The above thirteen steps have been written based on experiences that families have had with addicted family members. In view of this, this chapter is from one family to another. It was also written with the intent of saving families from the daily painful and worrisome horrors of dealing with a family member plagued with the sickness of addiction.

CHAPTER XI

Where Families Can Go to Get Help for Addicted Family Members

D ATA SHOWS THAT opioid treatment works, and that many Americans who have undergone drug treatment remain sober. There are many ex-opioid addicts in our workforce who are sustaining themselves and their families in legal and nonaddictive ways. Many of our best drug counselors were at one time plagued with the sickness of addiction, living on the streets and struggling for their next fix. There are also many professional people that at one time were addicted and now have resumed their professional lives and are outstanding citizens of our communities. Matter of fact, it was ex-addicts who opened up the first community-based drug treatment centers in America in the late fifties and early sixties. Most of these were nonprofit corporations that survived at the beginning by holding fundraisers to open up and keep going. Eventually, the federal government, through their Early Treatment Prisons, the Office of Equal Opportunity (OEO), Health and Human Services Agency (HHS), and the National Addiction Rehabilitation Act (NARA), started slowly funding some of these abovementioned nonprofit corporations. Presently, the federal government counts a very capable agency by the name of Substance Abuse and Mental Health Services Administration (SAMHSA) that funds local community-based drug treatment, prevention, and recovery programs.

At the beginning, trust levels had to be established with the addicted population. Since drugs are against the law, the addicted population was of the understanding that drug programs worked directly with law enforcement. Federal public laws dealing with confidentiality to protect addicts in treatment accomplished a great deal in developing that needed trust. Once the trust was established and the addicts felt that they were not going to be arrested for going into treatment, thousands and thousands of American addicts, many war veterans, went to treatment. These mentioned nonprofit programs became very successful and very well known nationally, and there was this passion to make America drug free. Other than developing their own successful treatment models, these pioneers developed highly effective outreach projects. In essence, they went to the addict and dealt with her/him in their own environment, in their own dialect, and as peers.

Government-funded outpatient clinics, residential treatment centers, and halfway houses were opened in every major city at the beginning, and we still find them operating today as they have evolved. The following is a brief description of these centers and how families may use these to assist an addicted family member.

1. Outpatient clinics are centers where an individual may go for addiction treatment, which consist of individual/group counseling/family counseling, medical detox from opioids, and/or long-term maintenance. The different types of counseling are usually given three to five times per week to individuals and/or their families in a group or individual basis. Most of these clinics also offer recovery services, which usually consist of an ex-addict or one in recovery helping the addict transition back into the community by assisting in job development, obtaining housing, and other benefits offered by other community agencies. Some of these outpatient clinics offer medically assisted treatment for the addicts who want to detox or be admitted into a medically assisted maintenance program. Methadone, Buprenorphine, and naltrexone are the most used medications that most doctors prefer to treat opioid addicts with or to maintain them for an extended period of time. The usual amount of time these outpatient clinics spend detoxing an addict depends on the addiction severity of the person, but it is usually done in a period of a week or two.

Methadone, being the most widely used medication for opioid addicts, is given to the addict in a de-escalating amount. In other words, once the addict is medically stabilized then the methadone is decreased, with some doctors using placebos. The placebo treatment is when the doctor medically detoxes the addict but does not tell her/him, continuing to give her/

him what resembles the medication when in reality it might be a sugar tablet. This is done to prove that the addict can do without the drug and control her/his craving. Eventually the addict is told that s/he has been off the medication for a period of time, which proves that there is no need for the continuation of the medicine. The addict at this time is informed that the treatment has been a success.

On the other hand, medically assisted maintenance consists of the doctor keeping the individual on medication for an extended period of time, usually months, and in some cases longer. The maintenance treatment is usually for hardcore opioid addicts who have been addicted to opioids for years.

The abovementioned treatments are usually free of charge and government funded; however, some do charge a minimal amount based on ability to pay or what is called a sliding fee scale.

2. Inpatient treatment is where an individual addict admits himself/herself or is admitted by the family and/or the courts and undergoes intensive treatment. The person usually lives at the center and only leaves the center to go to medical appointments, to see the probation officer, for employment reasons, and other limited reasons, but never is allowed to leave during detox. Detoxification is usually offered in the inpatient setting, especially for opioid addicts. The detox phase usually lasts from four to six days, followed by up to an average of three months of continuous psychological

treatment. There are some inpatient treatment programs that specialize in thirty-day treatment episodes.

Upon successfully completing inpatient treatment, the person is referred to an outpatient clinic for follow-up and after-care services, with the goal of avoiding relapse. There are government-funded inpatient treatment centers in every major city in America that offer no-charge services. However, most will charge a minimal amount based on ability to pay. There are also private for-profit hospitals in most major cities that also offer inpatient detox and thirty-day treatment programs. These hospitals serve addicts who carry health insurance that cover addiction treatment and/or have the ability to pay. Just like the nonprofit treatment programs, private hospitals also do excellent treatment for those in need.

3. There is a need for an explanation of the concepts of "cold turkey" and "maintenance" regarding an opioid addict. Cold turkey is when an opioid addict breaks the opioid addiction on her/his own without the assistance of any kind of medicine and/or doctor or treatment program. This usually takes three to four days of sweats, diarrhea, cramping, fevers, and the withdrawal feels like an intense bout with the flu. Cold turkey is usually not recommended for somebody that has a history of seizures, epilepsy, heart problems, and other sensitive medical conditions.

Actual detoxification is where the addict withdraws from his opioid addiction with the use of such medicines as methadone, naltrexone, Buprenorphine, and other medications as may be needed to treat other symptoms that may arise. Detoxification must be administered under the supervision of a medical doctor in every case. This is often called "medically assisted treatment."

"Maintenance" is also considered medically assisted treatment, and the same medications used in the detox are used in the maintenance, but usually maintenance is done for an extended period of time, where the addict goes and picks up his medication on a daily basis and must take it in the presence of medical staff. At times, in advance treatment, an addict is allowed "take home medication" for a designated amount of days. Maintenance is usually done for opioid addicts who have been addicted for many years, as was prior mentioned.

4. "Faith-based" treatment programs are also very much in existence presently. Most often these do not use medically assisted treatment but accept these referrals if the need is there, and usually accept the individual back after the medical treatment is finalized. This type of program concentrates on spiritual treatment on an outpatient and halfway house basis. Addicted family members may go to some of these programs several times per week or go live there 24/7. These are very good programs for people who are or may want to be and learn how to be spiritually driven. These

programs do not charge for their services, but will accept donations from actual patients or others.

5. Recovery services are usually offered by outpatient clinics and inpatient treatment centers. These services are given by ex-addicts and/or community volunteers. As explained in prior text, these services consist of job development, job training, obtaining housing, applying for food stamps and Medicare/Medicaid, obtaining clothing, transportation, and other supplemental services as may be needed by the addict and/or the family.

6. Alcoholics Anonymous (AA) and Narcotics Anonymous (NA) are recommended before any type of treatment, during and after. These are very strong support groups and spiritually guided efforts that have helped addicts since the beginning of time. These support group treatment components are probably the oldest treatment for addiction in America. AA and NA allow the addict to follow solid steps to full and lasting recovery. AA and NA have been known as major factors in preventing relapse. Daily attendance is highly recommended, as well as obtaining a sponsor to guide the addict in the recovery process. Most often sponsors arc individuals that are drug-free addicts and alcoholics in recovery themselves. There is no formal charge to join an AA or an NA group; however, donations are accepted.

7. Natural healing and alternatives are becoming more and more popular as people are realizing that many prescription medications can be very addictive. To reiterate, the approximately 90,000 recent overdose deaths per year in America have been attributed by some sources to opioid prescriptions. Hemp cannabidiol (CBD), as has been mentioned in prior chapters, is perhaps the most popular nonaddictive natural healing of the day. Much research has been done and more is needed, but as of late, CBD has been determined to be a good natural healer of opioid addiction in that it blocks the craving for the drug, plus heals many of the withdrawal symptoms, consisting of pain, inflammation, vomiting, diarrhea, fevers, shakes, sweats, and in severe cases, prevents or minimizes the severity of seizures. Regarding seizures, many parents have reported that CBD reduces the number of epileptic seizures and their intensity in their children (Devinsky O. Et Al., "Cannabidiol: Pharmacology And Potential Therapeutic Role In Epilepsy And Other Neuropsychiatric Disorders," *Epilepsia*: June 2014, 55 (6) 791-802).

Other natural healing alternatives are herbs of different types, physical therapy, flaming, bear bile, stone massages, spiritual healing, acupuncture, hormone replacement, etc.

Presently, there are many places where a family may go to find help, locally as well as statewide and nationally. The different types of services mentioned in this chapter are not all inclusive in that there are many other alternatives that are being explored and studied. The following chapter will deal with some cases and where families have gone for help, and what have been some of the results of using CBD as part of their treatment.

If you are desperate and cannot find treatment, call the national drug office named the Substance Abuse and Mental Health Services Administration (SAMHSA).

CHAPTER XII

Five Success Stories of Families Dealing with Opioid Addiction

THERE ARE MANY success stories of families dealing successfully with opioid addiction within their own family. The following five different stories are being offered as examples of how some families have won their fight against the plaguing sickness of opioid addiction using CBD.

STORY NUMBER I: A was fourteen when he started stealing Oxycodone, a synthetic opioid, from his grandmother. By the time he reached fifteen years of age, he had already become an opioid addict, was stealing from his family, was smoking marijuana regularly, had suffered two opioid overdoses and had been revived with NARCAN spray, had[25] the street smarts of a thirty-year-old, and was buying and selling Oxycodone on the streets. The family did intervention after intervention on A, but nothing seemed to work. The hysterical mother finally Googled drug treatment and got the address and phone number of a local government-funded drug treatment program. The program sent a twenty-year-old recovering addict to do an intervention with A. The recovering addict had a similar drug history as A, but he had been clean for four years and was dedicating his life to helping others. The interventionist was very successful, and convinced A to go into inpatient detox. During his thirty days at the treatment center, A relapsed once and escaped twice, but was able to bounce back. And now, he has been drug free for seven years. A is now a very successful drug prevention specialist at the same program that helped him. He specializes in helping youth. He finished his GED and is going to college, studying psychology. He still attends a support group on a weekly basis, and is taking CBD for anxiety and for that craving he still feels from time to time.

STORY NUMBER II: B grew up without a father and had a heroin addict for a mother. It was only the two of them. Her mother was a beautiful lady, and being addicted to the heroin, started selling her body to keep up with the $300 per day habit. The heroin addiction finally caught up with B's mother and she lost a lot of weight, contracted different sexually transmitted diseases, and became very sick and unattractive. B by this time had become a very attractive young lady of fifteen, and her mother, to keep up with her heroin addiction, manipulated her naive B into making money through prostitution. After a couple of years of B prostituting herself, B's mother died of a heroin overdose. And by that time B was already addicted to Fentanyl, a synthetic opioid. Soon thereafter, B, being young and naive, suffered a near-fatal Fentanyl overdose herself, and at the same time was charged with prostitution and possession of a controlled substance. And being a first-time offender, B was court ordered into a public-funded drug treatment program and given three years' probation. After treatment, B went to live with her grandparents. B, right after treatment, joined

Alcoholic Anonymous (AA), got married, had two children, and is a marketing director, and uses CBD for anxiety and craving.

STORY NUMBER III: C was the son of a rich father who was considered a leader in the community. His mother was a socialite and would go from meeting to meeting. In view of this, C and his brothers grew up on their own with little or no supervision. This being the case, the three of them started smoking marijuana at the age of ten, and by the age of twelve, C was already addicted to "speedballing," which is a combination of heroin and cocaine. C was also a poly-drug abuser; that is, he would do whatever drug he could get his hands on. His family, once they found out that he was addicted, admitted him to private treatment and paid a lot of money. He would be successful for a while, then relapse and would get addicted again. C complained of his constant craving for the drugs. After having tried different types of treatment, his grandmother finally recommended that he go to a naturalist who uses herbs in treatment along with conventional medicine. After detoxing with conventional medicine and the herb oil CBD for his craving and anxiety, C felt as if the cravings and anxiety had gone away. Presently, C continues to use CBD daily and has become quite functional in his life. He presently owns and manages a medium-sized construction company and has been drug free for over ten years. C also attends a support group meeting weekly for Christian men. He is presently married and has two children and a lovely and supportive wife.

STORY NUMBER IV: D was married to E, a beautiful lady who was a drug counselor. D had smoked marijuana on weekends but never considered himself an addict. E knew of his marijuana smoking and would complain to D about it. E, after a while, started noticing that D was losing a lot of weight and seemed quite anxious at times. E finally confronted him and D admitted to being addicted to synthetic opioids, which started when he was prescribed some of them for pain as a result of a back injury. Furthermore, he told E that as a medical sales representative he had been using synthetic opioids for over ten years, supporting his habit by stealing from his company. E finally convinced him to go through outpatient methadone detox, but after a month he relapsed.

He attempted detox again, and again he relapsed. Finally, the detox doctor recommended using the slow-dissolving naltrexone implant in the abdomen for six months. This worked for three months, but D relapsed, took some Oxycontin synthetic opioids, and became violently sick. D found out that naltrexone, being an antagonist drug, will cause sickness if opioids are taken while on that medication. A heart condition was discovered at that point; therefore, the doctor switched him to Buprenorphine rod implants under his upper arm for six months. The doctor switched because Buprenorphine does not cause sickness when mixed with opioids. During those six months and after the trauma of his violent sickness, D never relapsed again. D has been clean and drug free for three years, and he and his wife are now expecting their first child. He is back at work and is consulting with a drug counselor once per week. And of course, his wife E, a well-respected drug counselor herself, keeps an eagle eye on him, and is very proud of her husband being drug free, and has him taking CBD for his craving.

STORY NUMBER V: A mother frantically calls 911 and states that her daughter, F, can't breathe and that she has been vaping. F is rushed to the hospital, where she is stabilized and sent home, where she confesses to her mother. Apparently, she had been putting in synthetic opioids into her vape pen. She further confessed that she had been taking Fentanyl opioids for over a year, and that she has been selling also to support her habit.

The mother had already suspected opioid abuse but was in shock, and got onto the computer and Googled drug abuse treatment. She came up with the Substance Abuse and Mental Health Services Administration (SAMHSA) and accessed the www.samhsa.gov website, where she was able to find the phone numbers and addresses of all the government-funded drug programs in her region.

While the mother was on the computer, F went into her room and her hidden stash. The opioid craving was so intense that she took a large dose of Fentanyl and overdosed on the spot.

After being on the phone with a local drug program counselor and getting an appointment for F, the mother hung up and went to F's room and found her unresponsive, and immediately suspects a Fentanyl overdose. Having suspected opioid abuse and having seen it on TV, the mother had gone to the drugstore and bought a NARCAN spray. She immediately sprayed it into each nostril.

After what seemed like an eternity, F responded and started thrashing on the floor and finally woke up. At which time the mother called 911 again. F was kept at the hospital for three days and transferred to the local government-funded detox program, where she underwent methadone detox for four days.

After undergoing detox and a twenty-day residential treatment program, F went home. After being at home for a week, she ran off with her boyfriend, and the family, being in debt paying for F's treatment and emotionally drained, decided to allow her to "hit rock bottom." After several other overdoses, a couple of trips to jail, F's boyfriend passing away from a Fentanyl overdose, being homeless, F showed up at home and met with both her mother and father and told them she had contracted HIV-AIDS and wanted to come home finally. The mother and father accepted her with open arms and immediately enrolled F in a government-funded drug treatment program that deals with HIV patients.

F has been drug free for over AIDS treatment, is in a college working on her doctorate degree. In the meantime, F has a nine-year-old brother who was born with epilepsy, and as a result of him taking CBD, his seizures have almost disappeared. F, knowing and seeing the effects of CBD on her brother, decided to take CBD for her anxiety, and that also is almost gone. Presently, F is a very well-known grief counselor and enjoying her newfound life.

Just like there are over 90,000 opioid overdoses per year in America, there are also many success stories such as the five presented above. The message here is that through intervention, education, treatment, and recovery the opioid epidemic will be defeated. Through innovative and creative healers like CBD and others, and the family will lead the way, because it is the American family that is at the frontline and the most affected!

America finds itself in a very awkward situation where well-known medications have gone from being healers to killers and devastators of families. According to extensive experience in the healing of addictions, the time is now to revert to natural remedies that heal and don't kill. CBD might be this comprehensive start. Many American families swear by it!

The statements in this handbook have not been evaluated by the Food and Drug Administration. The information in this handbook is not intended to diagnose, treat, cure, or prevent any disease, but simply share experiences, opinions, and existing research regarding cannabidiol (CBD), which many Americans consider a natural alternative to healing opioid addiction as an answer to the existing opioid epidemic in America that has already claimed hundreds of thousands of American lives.

CHAPTER XIII

Latest Research Claiming CBD Works in the Treatment of Opioid Addiction

THERE IS A lot of research and study that seem to conclude that CBD works well in the treatment of opioid addiction. These studies have shown very positive results and have scientifically proven that CBD has some healing value. A perfect example is a recent study entitled "Cannabidiol for the Reduction of Cue-Induced Craving and Anxiety in Drug Abstinent Individuals with Heroin Use Disorder: A Double-Blind Randomized Placebo-Control Old Trail" published in the *American Journal of Psychiatry*, 2019, by Y. L. Hurd, S. Spriggs, J. Alishayvev, G. Winkel, K. Gurgov, C. Kudich, and E. Salsitz, which clearly points out scientifically that CBD assists in the treatment of opioid addiction. Dr. Yasmin Hurd, who is the director of the Addiction Institute at Mount Sinai, led the study and is a professor in pharmacological sciences, neuroscience, and psychiatry, and counts many years in the study of neurobiology underlying addiction disorders and is well published in the field.

The mentioned study was a very simple clinical trial that included forty-two participants, all of whom were addicted to opioids or had a recent history of addiction. These forty-two participants were divided into three groups. One group was given 400 mgs of CBD daily for three days. The second group was given 800 mgs of CBD, also for three days. And the third group was given a fake pill for three days, containing no CBD, otherwise known as a placebo. Immediately after the third day, twenty-four hours after, and seven days after, all participants were measured for the following: 1.) opioid craving, 2.) anxiety, 3.) positive and negative emotions, 4.) vital signs (body temperature, blood pressure and heart rate, and respiratory rate), and 5.) stress response. Before being measured, all participants were exposed to videos showing addicts injecting themselves with heroin and using opioids by sniffing it through their nostrils. Immediately after the videos, the participants were exposed to heroin-related paraphernalia (syringes, rubber ties, and packets of powder resembling heroin).

The results of the above stated factors measured at the mentioned three stages were very conclusive:

1. Participants receiving CBD showed less craving than those receiving the placebo.

2. The less-craving effect lasted for CBD dose.

3. It also showed that CBD reduced stress response, such as heart rate.

4. Participants receiving CBD reported less anxiety compared to those receiving the placebo.

5. No effect was noted by the CBD users on positive effects or on any cognitive measures.

In short, this small but significant study clearly shows that CBD reduces craving and anxiety in opioid-addicted individuals, and most experts have concluded that these two factors are of the utmost importance in dealing with opioid addiction. Any parent, wife, or relative that has dealt with an opioid-addicted family member or friend can also attest to the fact that craving and anxiety are very important factors in people getting sick with an addictive disorder and/or relapsing, many times right after having undergone inpatient and outpatient treatment and recovery.

Finally, it is very clear that CBD should play an important role in the overall treatment of opioid addiction, especially as it relates to relapse prevention of the opioid use disorder. It is also the belief that every home, after consulting with the family doctor, should have NARCAN to deal with possible overdose, and CBD to deal with relapse prevention. In today's world that is experiencing thousands of overdose deaths each year, CBD should be complementing not just NARCAN but also other effective opioid treatment medications like methadone, Buprenorphine, and others on the market.

It is also time to become aggressive with the use of other natural remedies that have proven to be effective for many generations. Lastly, it is a strong belief that we need to again develop aggressive outreach projects that will go out to where the opioid addict lives and bring her/him into treatment, rather than waiting for the referral. Aggressive outreach that is innovative, performed by persons in recovery is a great need in our battle against the opioid addiction epidemic. Families also need to play an aggressive role in this outreach; in other words, an army of aggressive outreach workers is very much needed to prevent the continuation of thousands of more deaths.

After reading this handbook and looking at the research presented, and if you are of the belief that hemp CBD can be good at healing the opioid addiction illness and/or other illnesses, then before proceeding, take into consideration the following seven factors:

1. Listen to the FDA and consult your health services provider before using any hemp CBD product.

2. Use CBD that is derived only from the hemp plant.

3. Study and ask how the hemp CBD you are going to use was extracted. Beware and be very cautious of CBD that was chemically extracted (study Chapter IV of the handbook).

4. Consult your healthcare provider and study the proper dosage for the illness of opioid addiction and any other ailment that you are going to use CBD for as a healing agent.

5. Consult with your family doctor as to how you, a family member, or a friend will administer the CBD, in that there is a significant difference in eating a CBD Gummy Bear and placing CBD oil under the tongue, and all the other forms of administering CBD. CBD in doping pens is seriously not recommended.

6. Do not buy CBD off the streets. If you do so, you will never really know what you are buying. If you are going to buy CBD, buy it from a business that is regulated by the state and federal government as per the state and federal farm bills. There have been cases where street CBD is laced with the powerful and deadly synthetic opioid Fentanyl and other substances that can be very detrimental to your health.

7. It is highly recommended not to use Delta-8 CBD or Delta-8 THC. CBD experts state that Delta-8 is lab made, and that it is not natural. It is also known that long before Delta-8, there were lab technicians who were using chemical conversion methods to produce synthetic drugs that were very powerful and created many health problems. It must be noted that converting hemp CBD into Delta-8 requires the use of very dangerous solvents like alkanes and heptane. To worsen the health threat, after the deadly solvents there are acids that are also used. Some of these acids used are alumina acid, sulfonic acid, and hydrochloric acid. The problem here is that all these solvents and acids leave dangerous residual chemicals in the CBD, such

as acetic acid. The result is that if acetic acid is ingested or inhaled, it can be very dangerous to the health of a person. Recently, realizing the dangers of Delta-8, state health departments are clarifying that Delta-8 is illegal. Even the Drug Enforcement Administration (DEA) has recently clarified that synthetically derived Delta-8, even though it might contain .3 percent or less of THC as per the law, is still illegal and is considered a Schedule I controlled substance similar to heroin, LSD, Extasy, and so on.

Lastly, it must be noted that the FDA and the CDC are receiving adverse-event reports regarding Delta-8 users. These reports consist of Delta-8 users who have been rushed to the hospital for emergency room services right after using Delta-8. Some of these adverse events have included vomiting, hallucinations, trouble standing, loss of consciousness, etc. In addition to the FDA and CDC reports, the US Poison Control Centers have reported 660 exposure to Delta-8 cases in the first seven months of the 2021 calendar year. The point here is do not be led into using CBD or THC. The chemicals used to convert CBD into Delta-8 can be deadly.

REFERENCES

3 Tips for Picking the Right CBD. http://www.CBDMD.com.

Ahmad, Farid. *CDC's National Center for Health Statistics.*

Bitencourt R.M. and R. N. Takahashi. 2018. Cannabidiol as a Therapeutic Alternative for Post-Traumatic Stress Disorder: From Bench Research in Human Trials. *Front Neurosci* 12, (July 24, 2018): 502.

Blessing, Ester M. et al. 2015. Cannabidiol as a Potential Treatment for Anxiety Disorders. *Neurotherapeutics* 12, 4 (October): 825–836.

Briefing Opioids, The Death Curve. *The Economist*, February 23, 2019.

Crippa, Jose A., Francisco S. Guimaraes, Alline C. Campos, and Antonio W. Zuardi. 2018. Translational Investigation of the Therapeutic Potential of Cannabidiol (CBD): Toward A New Age. *Frontiers in Immunology* (September).

D'ammassa, Algernon. Hemp Company Opens Near Las Cruces, Promises 180 Jobs. *Las Cruces Sun News*, USA Today Network, Texas, El Paso Times, May 28, 2019

Datsuyama, S. et al. 2013. Involvement of Peripheral Cannabinoid and Opioid Receptors In B-Caryophllene-Induced Antinociception. *Eur J Pain* 17, 5 (May): 664–75.

Devinsky, O. et al. 2014. Cannabidiol Pharmacology and Potential Therapeutic Role in Epilepsy and Other Neuropsychiatric Disorders. *Epilepsia* 55, 6: 791–802.

Drug Enforcement Administration (DEA), Automation of Reports and Consolidated Orders System (ARCOS), Drug Data Collection System.

FDA Approves Six Month Implant for Treatment of Opioid Dependence (Long Acting, Subdermal Buprenorphine Called Probuphine Implant, Medicated Rods). National Institute on Drug Abuse (NIDA) announcement, May 26, 2016.

FDA Moves Quickly to Approve Easy to Use Nasal Spray to Treat Opioid Overdose (Naloxone = Narcan). FDA New Release, November 18, 2015.

Guimaraes, F. S., J. C. De Aguiar, R. Mechoulam, and A. Breuer. 1994. Anxiolytic Effect of Cannabidiol Derivatives in the Elevated Plus - Maze, Gen Pharmacol. *Pub Med*, Google Scholar 25, 1: 161–4.

Gwin, Peter. 2019. The Secrets of Chinese Medicine. *National Geographic* January.

Hurd, Y. L., S. Spriggs, J. Alishayvev, G. Winkel, K. Gurgov, C. Kudich, and E. Salsitz. 2019. Cannabidiol for the Reduction of Cue Induced Craving and Anxiety in Drug Abstinent Individuals with Heroin Use Disorder: A Double-Blind Randomized Placebo Controlled Trial. *American Journal of Psychiatry*.

Hurd, Y. L. et al. 2015. Early Phase in the Development of Cannabidiol as a Treatment for Addiction: Opioid Relapse Takes Initial Center Stage. *Neurotherapeutics* 4 (October): 807–15.

Katsidoni V., I. Anagnostou, and G. Panagis. 2013. Cannabidiol Inhibits the Reward Facilitating Effect of Morphine: Involvement Of 5-HT1A Receptors in the Dorsal Raphe Nucleus. *Addict Biol* 18, 2: 286–96.

Koop, G. F. and N. D. 2010. Volkow. Neuro-Circuitry of Addiction. *Neuropsychopharmacology* 35, 1: 217–38.

Kraft, Daniel. 2019. The Future of Medicine. *National Geographic* January.

Mayo Clinic. CBD Dosage Recommendations, 2018.

———. CBD Dosages Based on Scientific Research, January 2019.

Morgan, C.J., R. K. Das, A. Joye, H. V. Curran, and S. K. Kamboj. 2013. Cannabidiol Reduces Cigarette Consumption in Tobacco Smokers: Preliminary Findings. *Addict Behav* 38, 9:2433–6.

Nachtivey, James. 2018. The Opioid Diaries. *Times Magazine* March 5.

Perrault, Abbie. 2019. Village Farm Has High Hopes for Hemp in Far West Texas. *The Big Bend Sentinel*, June 6.

Prud'homme, Melissa et al. 2015. Cannabidiol as an Intervention for Addictive Behaviors: A Systematic Review of the Evidence. *Substance Abuse* 9: 33–38.

Rawls, Bill. 2019. The Science Behind CBD Oil: Everything You Need To Know. January 30.

Ren Y., L. Whittard, A. Higuerra-Mattas, C. V. Morris, and Y. L. Hurd. 2009. Cannabidiol, A Non-Psychotropic Component of Hemp, Inhibits Cue-Induced Heroin Seeking and Normalizes Discrete Mesolimbic Neuronal Disturbances. *Journal Of Neuroscience*.

Roberts, J. J. 2018. Red Staters See Green in Hemp. *Fortune* July 1.

Russo, E. B., A. Burnett, B. Hall, and K. K. Parker. 2006. Agonistic Properties of Cannabidiol at 5-HT1A Receptors. *Neurochemistry Research*.

Schoedel, K. A. et al. 2018. Abuse Potential Assessment of Cannabidiol (CBD) in Recreational Polydrug Users: A Randomized Blind Controlled Trial. *Epilepsy Behav 88* (October): 162–171.

Stoble, M. 2019. Overdose Deaths Seem to Slip in 2018. *Associated Press* January.

Texas Farm Bill, House Bill 1325, June 2019 (Governing Hemp)

Thomas, A., G. L. Baille, A. M. Phillips, R. K. Razdan, R. A. Ross, and R. G. Pertwee. 2007. Cannabidiol Displays Unexpected High Potency as an Antagonist of CB1 and CB2 Receptor Agonist in Vitro. *Br J Pharmacol* 150, 5: 613–23.

Tomida, I, A. Azuara-Blanco, H. House, M. Flint, R.G. Pertwee, and P. J. Robson. 2006. Effect of Sublingual Application of Cannabidiol on Intra Ocular Pressure: A Pilot Study. *J. Glucoma*.

Use Opioid Medications to Save Lives (Methadone, Naltrexone, and Buprenorphine). *El Paso Times*. April 6, 2019.

Zanelati T.V., C. Biojone, F. A. Moreira, F. S. Guimaraes, and S. R. Joca. 2010. Antidepressant-Like Effects of Cannabidiol in Mice: Possible Involvement of 5-HT1A Receptors. *Br J Pharmacol* 159, 1: 122–8.

NOTES ON THE AUTHOR

J OSE JONES, THE author of this handbook, counts many years in the field of opioid addiction treatment. He started as a peer opioid addiction counselor in 1960s. By the late sixties he was in Vietnam, and as a decorated combat medic, performed opioid overdose treatment. After the war he finished his graduate work at a university and worked as an opioid addiction counselor for a private hospital, and eventually worked at a drug treatment and prevention agency in the drug treatment arena until he became the executive director and worked there for forty years. During his almost five decades of working in the opioid treatment field, he received many awards, including a national citation by the Public Health Service and designation to a national opioid expert panel by the Feds. In 2011 he was sent to federal prison, where he taught drug addiction treatment to other inmates.

Jose Jones believes that treatment works, and that CDB also works and should be used to supplement and complement existing science-based and best practice treatment.